THE **MISSING ELEMENT** OF
WORSHIP

WHAT'S *Love* GOT TO DO WITH IT?

TOM KRAEUTER

Emerald Books
P.O. BOX 635, LYNNWOOD, WA 98046

Emerald Books are distributed through YWAM Publishing. For a full list of titles, visit our website at www.ywampublishing.com or call 1-800-922-2143.

The Missing Element of Worship:
What's Love Got to Do with It?
Copyright © 2007 Training Resources, Inc.
8929 Old LeMay Ferry Road
Hillsboro, MO 63050
(636) 789-4522
www.training-resources.org

12 11 10 09 08 07   10 9 8 7 6 5 4 3 2 1

ISBN-13: 978-1-932096-52-1
ISBN-10: 1-932096-52-3

Published by Emerald Books
P.O. Box 635
Lynnwood, Washington 98046

Library of Congress Cataloging-in-Publication Data
Kraeuter, Tom, 1958–
  The missing element of worship : what's love got to do with it? / by Tom Kraeuter.
    p. cm.
  Includes bibliographical references and index.
  ISBN-13: 978-1-932096-52-1 (pbk. : alk. paper)
  ISBN-10: 1-932096-52-3 (alk. paper)
  1. Church. 2. Love–Religious aspects–Christianity. 3. Concord. 4. Community–Religious aspects–Christianity. 5. Forgiveness of sin. 6. Worship. I. Title.
  BV600.3.K73 2007
  264—dc22   2007033493

Unless otherwise noted, all Scripture quotations are from the Holy Bible, English Standard Version, copyright © 2001 by Crossway Bibles, a division of Good News Publishers. Used by permission. Verses marked NIV are taken from the New International Version® of the Bible, copyright © 1973, 1978, 1984 by the International Bible Society. Used by permission. All rights reserved. All italicized words in Scripture quotes are author's emphasis.

All rights reserved. No part of this publication may be reproduced, stored in a retrieval system, or transmitted, in any form or by any means, electronic, mechanical, photocopying, recording, or otherwise, without the prior written permission of the publisher.

Printed in the United States of America.

OTHER BOOKS BY TOM KRAEUTER

Becoming a True Worshiper

Keys to Becoming an Effective Worship Leader

Guiding Your Church Through a Worship Transition

Developing an Effective Worship Ministry

Things They Didn't Teach Me in Worship Leading School

Worship Is…What?!

*If Standing Together Is So Great,
Why Do We Keep Falling Apart?*

*Oh, Grow Up!
The Everyday Miracle of Becoming More Like Jesus*

Times of Refreshing: A Worship Ministry Devotional

Are There Terrorists in Your Church?

THANKS TO:

Thanks to the thousands of Christians who are living the scriptural mandate to love one another. I frequently see the lives and hear the stories as I travel. It is from you that I gained the inspiration to write this book.

Thanks to Emerald Books for having enough confidence in my writing to publish another book.

Special thanks to Jennifer Brody for another great editing job.

And, of course, thanks to my family—Barbara, David, Stephen, and Amy—for loving me all the way through the time-consuming writing of another book.

I humbly dedicate this book to my daughter, Amy.

Amy, your love for people makes this a perfect book for me to dedicate to you.

I thoroughly enjoy having you as my daughter. Our frequent hand-in-hand Sunday morning walks have been a small piece of heaven here on earth for me. Your smile and laughter warm this dad's heart in ways you can't even imagine now.

Without a doubt, I am very glad that the Lord placed you in our family.

Contents

1. Setting the Stage 9
2. Love One Another 15
3. Constructing the Temple 25
4. Destroying the Temple 35
5. Two Very Different Churches 41
6. Unity, Not Uniformity 51
7. What's So Important about Unity? 55
8. Creating an Honest Sense of Community 63
9. Love Unconditionally 75
10. Forgive as the Lord Forgave You 83

   Epilogue 89

   Notes 93

1.

SETTING THE STAGE

ON A BEAUTIFUL spring morning, everyone was trickling in to New Heights Christian Church just before the late service began. Josalyn, a relatively new Christian, caught sight of David as he walked through the back door of the church. They had dated three times, all within the past couple of weeks. Unfortunately for Josalyn, David had decided that she wasn't the person with whom he wanted to spend the rest of his life, so he ended the relationship. Josalyn, on the other hand, had enjoyed their times together. She had begun to think that David would be a good catch. But now she was miffed. *What a slug,* she thought. *I can't believe he's still got the nerve to come to church.* She dramatically turned in her seat and faced the opposite direction.

Sonya and Bill sat just one row back but farther over on the same side of the church as Josalyn. "Look at that dress Josalyn is wearing," Sonya whispered with a tone of disgust. "No, better yet, don't look. It is much too tight for her to be wearing to church. She needs to get a clue."

"Where is she?" Bill whispered as he suddenly looked around.

"Never mind," his wife snapped.

Elmer and Gloria sat in the very back pew on the left, the same place they had sat every Sunday for the past forty-seven years. "If that kid starts banging on those drums again, I'm leaving," Elmer whispered loudly enough for those around him to hear. "I've about had it with that music." No one was quite sure if Elmer wanted others to hear or if Gloria didn't have her hearing aid turned up again.

Teenage friends Ben and Sam sat two-thirds of the way back on the right near the side door. They were uncharacteristically quiet this particular morning. Quiet, that is, until an overweight, elderly woman waddled down the main aisle. Ben nearly laughed out loud as Sam stood and began to imitate her walk. Fortunately she didn't see him, and a few sharp looks from those seated nearby put an end to the episode. Sam sat, but he and Ben continued their laughter. Worse, they murmured criticisms of others throughout the entire service.

Robert, a bank auditor by profession, sat alone on the opposite side. Robert—"Mr. Detail" his friends called him—knew that in the past two years Pastor Perkins's sermons had gone from 23 percent Scripture to just 15 percent. The pastor still used Scripture, but he used fewer verses and spent more time expounding on the verses he used. From Robert's perspective, however, an 8 percent drop in the amount of God's Word used was inexcusable. He checked his stopwatches once more to be sure he was ready for the sermon. He wanted to make certain he had complete and accurate information for the voters' meeting next Thursday night.

Just then Anne walked in with the baby in her arms and her other five straggling behind. The shabby dress of all seven spoke volumes about their financial situation. Rhonda leaned toward her husband and whispered, "Why does Anne always wear that same old dress week after week? She needs to get herself a better job, or maybe a new husband. He must be a real jerk. Have you ever seen him? Just look at all those kids. Margaret Schultz told me that they—" Rhonda went on for quite some time. Her husband just kept nodding and smiling, though he paid little attention to anything she said. Ever.

One of the ushers that day was a tall, muscular, handsome man named Zach. As he escorted beautiful—and eligible—Cynthia to her seat, Zach gently put his hand on her shoulder and confided, "Be ready. The pastor is really long-winded this morning." He shook his head as though in total disbelief. "The sermon took almost twenty-six minutes in the first service. I thought he'd never get done." Cynthia smiled coyly at Zach and thanked him for the information as she sat down near the end of the pew.

"Why does Zach *always* escort Cynthia to her seat?" Jane asked as she watched. "He's never once offered to escort me to *my* seat."

Her husband, Jim, looked at her curiously. In a low voice he asked, "Do I really need to answer that question?" He paused, then continued, "You're probably twenty years older than she is, and," Jim rolled his eyes as if stating the obvious, "she's single." Jim stared at his wife, amazed that Jane didn't seem to understand this. "Besides, why would you *want* him to escort you to your seat?"

"I just—" Anything else Jane said was drowned out by the opening notes of the organ prelude.

As the music began, each of the members quickly glanced through the bulletin, checking the songs and other information about the service. They all dutifully noted the sermon title, "Love One Another," but, interestingly, each person had the same reaction: *Why can't Pastor Perkins find something else to talk about? We have certainly heard that theme enough.*

Here's the question: As the Lord views this scene, what does *He* think? Is this an atmosphere conducive to worship? If you were God, would you want to be worshiped in the midst of such bickering and rivalry? Would you condone such negative attitudes and gossip? Are these godly characteristics?

When the people looked at the sermon title, "Love One Another," and thought, *We have heard that theme enough,* perhaps if they stopped to listen closely, they might have heard the Holy Spirit whisper, "Maybe you have heard it, but you have not done it."

You see, from God's perspective, the element frequently missing from our worship is *love for one another.*

WHAT'S REALLY IMPORTANT?

One day a man who was a Pharisee and an expert in the Torah asked Jesus, "Teacher, which is the great commandment in the Law?" (Matt. 22:36). That's a serious question, one that might require some forethought to be sure the answer is proper and accurate. Interestingly, Scripture does not indicate that Jesus hesitated even slightly before answering. Do you recall how He responded? "You shall love the Lord your God with all your heart and with all your soul and with all your mind. This is the

Setting the Stage

great and first commandment. And a second is like it: You shall love your neighbor as yourself" (Matt. 22:37–39).

Notice that Jesus was not asked about the second most important commandment. The inquiry was not, "Tell us the *two* most important commandments." No, only one was requested, but Jesus gave two as an answer. Looking at other answers Jesus gave when questions were asked of Him, it would seem to me that this answer offers more than appears on the surface. Jesus often gave more information than requested, but the information was always germane. He didn't throw in additional topics just to lengthen the conversation. Jesus didn't speak in order to hear Himself talk. He always chose His words very carefully and made His point as effectively as possible. In light of this, Jesus apparently sees these two issues—relationship with God and relationship with one another—as interrelated. In His mind these are not separate subjects. They are intrinsically connected.

The apostle Peter says, "*Above all,* keep loving one another earnestly" (1 Pet. 4:8). "Above all" sounds pretty important. But don't get the wrong idea here. Peter is not reversing the order of the two greatest commandments. By the time Peter wrote these words, his relationship with God was primary. Much of this letter prior to the fourth chapter concerns our relationship with the Lord. Once that foundation is in place, though, Peter builds on it, saying, "Above all, keep loving one another." Peter recognized the necessity of our relationship to one another in the context of our relationship to God.

The apostle Paul told the church at Colossae, "We always thank God, the Father of our Lord Jesus Christ, when we pray for you." Those are exciting words! How would you like to receive a letter from the apostle Paul saying that he thanked God every time he prayed for you? But Paul went on to explain why he thanked God: "since we heard of your faith in Christ Jesus and of the love you have for all the saints" (Col. 1:3-4). Paul was grateful for their faith in Christ and also for their love for one another. He was pleased that they had trusted Christ for their salvation *and* that they were learning to love each other.

Throughout the Bible, the two issues of primary importance are our relationship with God and our relationship with one another. It is vital to recognize that these two relationships are interconnected. You cannot love God without loving others. In other words, your relationships with your brothers and sisters in Christ will definitely affect your worship of God.

2.

LOVE ONE ANOTHER

JASON AND NICOLE fought incessantly. Though they were brother and sister, most people would never know it. From their earliest days they consistently antagonized one another. Not just arguments, but mean-spirited, nasty arguments. They had been at it so long that, at this point, they really didn't even like one another.

Born of the same parents, Jason and Nicole grew up in the same home, but that's where their similarities ended. Jason was an introvert. Shy, quiet, and extremely intelligent, he spent lots of time reading. Few things captured his interest more than learning. Perhaps the one real passion that did delight him more than learning was demonstrating his knowledge. Although Jason did not relish being in the limelight, he did enjoy debating with others. He could generally shred any argument an opponent threw his way. And shredding those arguments, especially with a few extra demeaning barbs thrown in, gave Jason a smug satisfaction like nothing else.

Nicole was quite different from her brother. Vivacious, outgoing, and friendly, she was everything that Jason was not. Nearly everyone was Nicole's friend. No matter where she went, her broad smile, personal charm, and fun-loving manner caused people to like her. Everyone except Jason. He envied her confident, effervescent ways. Secretly he wished he could be more like Nicole, but he couldn't. So he settled for humiliating her through their arguments. He knew that was the one area where he had an advantage.

Ron, Jason and Nicole's dad, mourned their incessant fighting. He was a Christian and tried everything he knew to get them to stop. He showed them what the Bible says about loving one another and being kind. He begged and pleaded with them not to belittle one another. He told them how much *he* wanted them to love one another—"Nothing makes my heart more proud as a father than when my children get along with each other." He told them stories of how getting along would make a positive difference in both their lives. However, none of these efforts seemed to make any long-term difference. The siblings continued their contentious quarreling at every opportunity.

Finally, one day when Nicole and Jason were in high school, they were squabbling yet again about some overblown trivial incident. Their words flew back and forth toward one another like arrows shot from a bow. Like expert archers, their aim was accurate, and the arrows hit the bull's-eye every time. The wounds inflicted were serious.

As they argued on, their father suddenly collapsed to the floor and began bawling like a baby. Ron drew his knees up to his chest and lay on the floor wailing in apparent pain. Jason and Nicole stopped their fighting and stared at their dad, but he kept on crying. They ran to him and tried to console him, but on and on he cried. Suddenly, when he caught his breath enough to speak, Ron complained of a sharp pain in his chest. Nicole immediately called 911. They tried to comfort him for what seemed like hours during the minutes until the rescue squad arrived. The EMTs did a preliminary check and quickly whisked Ron away.

Hours later, at the hospital, the attending physician came to the room where Nicole and Jason were waiting. He looked grave, and his tone was extremely serious. "Your father has had a heart attack. He is in *very* critical condition. We don't know for sure if he'll make it. Right now your dad seems to be hanging on by a thread." He paused to let the words sink in. "It's very strange, though. We can find no blockage in his arteries, and no deterioration of the heart in any way. None of the things that would generally trigger such an attack appear to be present. So it seems as though something else—some outside, major traumatic episode—must have caused the attack." He paused again, then continued. "What was your father doing when he collapsed?"

The teenagers sat silently. Both knew they were the cause of their father's heart attack. The doctor, thinking they were too shocked to respond, excused himself, leaving Jason and Nicole to their own thoughts.

Jason thought back to the many times he had seen the pained expression on his dad's face because of the arguing. *It's my fault,* he thought. *I didn't really* need *to argue. Certainly not if it meant killing Dad. How could I have been so stupid?* he wondered. Jason stared out the window of the hospital waiting room. His thoughts became prayers. *Lord, please forgive me. And would you heal my dad?*

Nicole had similar feelings racing through her mind. She recalled the many times their father had pled with them, "Please love one another." Their consistent, nasty bickering had caused such grief in her dad. All the stories he had told them—some original, others gleaned from various sources—flooded back into her brain. Some seemed silly. Regardless, they all had one main point: Don't fight; care for each other; love one another. Why hadn't she listened? Why had she waited until her father was teetering between life and death to realize how important this was? Her thoughts also turned to prayer. *God, please don't let my stupidity cause my dad any more pain. Please heal him and let him live.*

Let's be candid for a moment. Sometimes it takes a traumatic event—perhaps something as serious as the death or near-death of a loved one—to cause us to realize that we need to change. Though emotions run high in such scenarios, we actually see much more clearly those things that are really important. The day-to-day, life-as-usual activities are turned upside down, and true priorities come into focus.

A friend of mine accidentally wiped out some extremely important information from his computer hard drive. Prior to this incident, he would have extolled the virtues of backing up data. Now, however, he actually does it. Daily. His traumatic experience changed his actions.

How many times have we heard about the alcoholic or drug addict who reached bottom and suddenly realized what was happening? *I can't go on like this any longer.* Or what about the person in a tragic automobile accident who survives and—having been given a second chance at life—now has very different priorities? Real and lasting changes are often made as a result of such experiences. Yet why do we wait for such tragic experiences? Too frequently we know the right thing to do and yet refuse to do it. Like Jason and Nicole, we continue until some horrendous catastrophe causes us to take a fresh look and make practical changes.

LOVE ONE ANOTHER

Picture the scene. It is Jesus' final night with His disciples before going to the cross. He knows what is going to happen the next day. He also knows that because of the events that will take place the next day, the words He says that night will be etched solidly into the minds and onto the hearts of His followers. When they see Him mocked and beaten and crucified, His final words will ring loudly in their ears. Jesus is keenly aware that they will remember His last statements to them. So, in light of this, what did Jesus tell them that night before He went to the cross?

"A new commandment I give to you, that you *love one another*: just as I have loved you, you also are to *love one another*. By this all people will know that you are my disciples, if you *have love for one another*" (John 13:34–35). In just two sentences, Jesus tells them three times that they should love one another.

If I want to make a strong point with my children or an audience to whom I am speaking, I will repeat a statement for emphasis. The repetition helps drive the idea home. In essence I am saying, "Hey, this is really important!" Do you think there's a remote chance that by repeating Himself—actually saying it in three different ways—Jesus was telling His disciples that loving one another was really, really important?

I find it interesting that the Lord doesn't seem to excuse our discord for reasons like personality difference or political views. He still insists that we love one another. Two of Jesus' handpicked disciples, Simon the Zealot and Matthew the tax collector, were about as opposite as you could get in that society. The Zealots were pro-Israel in every sense of the word. They wanted to battle the Romans and drive those uncircumcised heathen from their land. The tax collectors, on the other hand, had, in essence, sold out to the Romans. Their job was to collect taxes from their fellow Hebrews and give the money to Rome. In Israel, Zealots and tax collectors were polar opposites. Picture an ultraconservative Republican sitting next to a passionate, far-left-wing Democrat. Or a fanatical socialist seated with a Wall Street tycoon. Ideologically, Simon and Matthew were about as far apart as possible. Jesus still insisted they love one another. And God insists on the same for you and me.

Honestly, at times my kids are as different as night and day. Their personalities are so diverse that it is sometimes hard for me to believe that they came from the same parents and have grown up in the same environment their entire lives. I have often wondered, *How can they be so radically different?* Yet, even with their differences, they demonstrate their love for one another in myriad ways. Their willingness to help one another and their consistent care and concern have often been an inspiration to me and to others. That's the way we should act in the body of Christ. Stop bickering. Stop stabbing one another with daggers made of words. When there is a disagreement, reconcile quickly. Don't stomp off to your room and pout or, worse yet, spread gossip and rumors about the other person. No! Members of God's family have been given a very clear directive from the Lord: love one another.

I am not suggesting that we should never argue. Unfortunately, that word has come to imply something different than it originally meant. The earliest origins of *argue* did not bear the negative connotation we know today. It is only in more recent times that arguing has been thought of as something angry or unkind. We can argue (i.e., give reasons for an opinion in order to support it, discuss something in all its aspects, or try to persuade somebody by giving reasons) in the church, but we must do it kindly, not in a mean-spirited way. Disagreements are no excuse to act vindictively. Even when we do not see eye to eye, we should still display genuine care and compassion for each other.

A Life Worthy of the Gospel

Recently I spent a few months studying the book of Philippians. I read, reread, and memorized, trying to gain as much insight as possible. As I mulled over the words and phrases packed into Paul's powerful, upbeat letter to the church at Philippi, one verse in particular stood out to me over and over, "Only let your manner of life be worthy of the gospel of Christ" (Phil. 1:27). What a statement! *Worthy* of the gospel of Christ. How could that ever be? How could I—how could you—how could any of us ever have a manner of life *worthy* of the death and resurrection of the Lord Jesus? And if we could, what would it look like?

Interestingly, Paul goes on to describe what it means to live a life worthy of the gospel, but he does not include the things I would expect. Paul does not talk about living a wholesome life so unbelievers will see how different we are from them. He says nothing about smoking cigarettes or drinking alcohol. He makes no mention of reading the Bible or praying or worshiping. No, instead Paul describes a life worthy of the gospel like this: "standing firm in one spirit, with one mind striving side by side for the faith of the gospel." That's powerful! "One spirit...one mind...side by side..." Those words don't need much interpretation.

From the unique perspective of the apostle Paul, a life that is worthy of the gospel is one that is united in heart and mind and purpose with brothers and sisters in Christ. Jesus died on the cross not only to reconcile us to God but also to reconcile us to one another. Therefore, a manner of life worthy of the gospel is a life that is united in tangible ways with our fellow Christians.

Paul says something very similar in his letter to the Ephesians. "I...urge you to walk in a manner worthy of the calling to which you have been called" (Eph. 4:1). Do you see it? It's the same idea that he expressed to the Philippians: walk *worthy* of your calling. Okay, Paul, but what does that look like? He goes on to tell us how to do it: "...with all humility and gentleness, with patience, bearing with one another in love, eager to maintain the unity of the Spirit" (Eph. 4:2–3).

Do you want to walk worthy of the calling to which you have been called? Be humble and gentle and patient in your interactions with one another. Bear with one another in love. Be eager to maintain the unity of the Spirit. That's a tall order but definitely one worth pursuing.

Some time ago I was preaching at a church on Sunday morning. The topic of my sermon was, in essence, loving one another. After the service, a man approached me and took issue with one of my points. I carefully showed him again what the Bible says about the specific point, but he quickly retorted, "I just don't believe that." I was stunned. You see, disagreeing with me is one thing. Disagreeing with God's Word is quite another. That is a very dangerous place to be. Noted author and pastor Charles Stanley said it like this:

> I will always give priority to what the Scriptures say over my experience. I will not interpret the Scripture through

my experience. To do so is dangerous. It elevates me to the place of judge and jury over the Bible. [Instead] I want God to conform my experience to the truth of His Word.[1]

We must not wait until some catastrophic event makes us recognize the error of our ways. God's Word clearly tells us what to do. There is no reason to wait. As Dr. Robert Webber said, "We need to live out theological conviction, rather than merely mouthing theological truths and never putting them into practice."[2]

It should not take a crisis to cause what we believe on the inside to be manifested on the outside. Our internal beliefs must become our external actions. Using Webber's terminology, we need to put theological truths into practice. The Bible says, "But be doers of the word, and not hearers only" (James 1:22).

At this point you might be thinking, *Hold on. I thought this book was about worship. You've hardly mentioned it. Where does that part come in?* Throughout Scripture an undeniable connection exists between worship and unity. Our relationships with our brothers and sisters in Christ clearly affect our relationship with God. Experientially and scripturally, there is no doubt that the two are intrinsically connected. Let's move on to the next chapter and take a look at what the Bible has to say about this vital connection.

3.

CONSTRUCTING THE TEMPLE

THE FIRST TIME Saul of Tarsus is mentioned in the Bible is in the book of Acts. Saul later becomes Paul the apostle, but he is initially introduced to us at the stoning of Stephen. The anti-Christian Jews were executing Stephen because of his perceived blasphemy. Scripture says, "Then they cast him out of the city and stoned him. And the witnesses laid down their garments at the feet of a young man named Saul" (Acts 7:58).

Saul of Tarsus looked approvingly on the execution of Stephen (see Acts 8:1). In fact, he quickly went beyond observing the death of Christians. He soon became a leader in the ensuing persecution. Believers were scattered throughout the region, and Saul of Tarsus was at the forefront of their maltreatment. "But Saul was ravaging the church, and entering house after house, he dragged off men and women and committed them to prison" (Acts 8:3).

In the very next chapter, we find that Saul is not just a leader in this vast persecution, but appears to be the primary impetus. "But Saul, still breathing threats and murder against the disciples of the Lord, went to the high priest and asked him for letters to the synagogues at Damascus, so that if he found any belonging to the Way, men or women, he might bring them bound to Jerusalem" (Acts 9:1–2).

In that place and time, Saul of Tarsus was the number one human enemy of the church. No doubt most believers would have wanted plenty of distance between themselves and this adversary. But then something happened. It was so powerful and profound that it changed not only Saul of Tarsus but also the shape of the church from that time until now. Saul had a personal encounter with the Lord Jesus Christ.

> Now as he went on his way, he approached Damascus, and suddenly a light from heaven flashed around him. And falling to the ground he heard a voice saying to him, "Saul, Saul, why are you persecuting me?" And he said, "Who are you, Lord?" And he said, "I am Jesus, whom you are persecuting.... Saul rose from the ground, and although his eyes were opened, he saw nothing (Acts 9:3–5, 8a).

Try to picture this scenario in your mind. A blinding camera light flashes. Or perhaps a gigantic lightning bolt, more powerful than any you or I have ever seen. We don't know exactly what happened, but Saul fell to the ground and went blind in the process. That's a *bright* flash.

So as Saul is on the ground, he hears a voice ask, "Why are you persecuting me?" The voice is apparently audible, but Saul can see nothing. Again, try to imagine this scene. It is logical that in Saul's mind, he was probably thinking, *Uh-oh, is this someone—maybe Stephen—coming back from the dead to haunt me? Or perhaps it's someone I've been tracking.*

Therefore Saul says, "Who are you, Lord?"

In the Greek, the word "Lord" does not necessarily mean *the* Lord. It is often simply a term of respect. We would liken it to our word "sir." Saul asked, "Who are you, sir?"

Then comes a most unexpected response. "I am Jesus, whom you are persecuting."

At this point Saul could have easily and accurately responded, "Jesus? I never even met you." Quite probably Saul never even saw Jesus during His visible earthly ministry.

More importantly, though, think about the ramifications of that phrase, "I am Jesus, whom you are persecuting." If you look at the story, Saul wasn't actually persecuting Jesus, just His followers. Undoubtedly, Saul never considered the possibility that his persecution might be directed toward Jesus. Saul was certain that Jesus was dead and gone. His followers were what he was going after. However, from Jesus' perspective, clearly it was more than that. The Lord has so connected Himself to His people that we become one with Him. When someone does something to us as the church, it is as though he is doing it to Jesus Himself.

Jesus said much the same thing when He talked about His return:

> Then the King will say to those on his right, "Come, you who are blessed by my Father, inherit the kingdom prepared for you from the foundation of the world. For I was hungry and you gave me food, I was thirsty and you gave me drink, I was a stranger and you welcomed me, I was naked and you clothed me, I was sick and

you visited me, I was in prison and you came to me." Then the righteous will answer him, saying, "Lord, when did we see you hungry and feed you, or thirsty and give you drink? And when did we see you a stranger and welcome you, or naked and clothe you? And when did we see you sick or in prison and visit you?" And the King will answer them, "Truly, I say to you, *as you did it to one of the least of these my brothers, you did it to me.*" (Matt. 25:34–40)

This is the positive side of the same principle. When someone does anything to one of God's children, it is as though she is doing it to God Himself. "Truly, I say to you, *as you did it to one of the least of these my brothers, you did it to me.*"

Jesus reiterated this idea in a slightly different way when He said, "Truly, truly, I say to you, whoever receives the one I send receives me, and whoever receives me receives the one who sent me" (John 13:20). As His people, we are more than just the *representation* of Christ here on earth. We are, in reality, His body (see 1 Corinthians 12:27).

When Jesus asked why Saul was persecuting Him, He meant exactly that. Saul was not simply antagonizing and killing Jesus' followers. From the Lord's perspective, the persecution was directed toward Him.

LET'S GET PERSONAL

We need to recognize that this is not just about outsiders doing something to one of us. This is not only a matter of non-Christians doing nasty things to Christians. When Jesus was speaking in the Matthew passage above, He was referring to "the righteous" (i.e., believers, Christians). Those people did kind deeds for "the least of these my brothers," and the king said, "You did it to me." Again, this is the positive aspect, but there is a negative side also. When we in the body of Christ do or say something—whether it is kind or malicious—toward another, it is the same as doing it to Jesus Himself.

Let's take this a step further and make it personal. Have you ever walked in to your corporate gathering of worship and thought (or said) something negative about a brother or sister in Christ? Perhaps you thought (or said) something like, "Look at Joe over there. I wish he'd grow up, get his hair cut, and act like a normal Christian." Or "There's Sue. I hope she doesn't start talking to me. She has got to be one of the strangest people I've ever met! I wish she would just keep her distance from me."

Maybe you can think of your own examples when you thought or said something similar. Perhaps, if you're like me, you can recall times when your thoughts or words toward your fellow believers were far worse than these. If so, what was the outcome? Whether you realized it or not, you put a wall between yourself and that person. Harboring negative attitudes toward one another in the body of Christ will hinder not only our relationships with one another, but ultimately it will hinder our worship of God. Let me explain.

In the second chapter of his letter to the Ephesians, Paul discusses the concept of the church being built together into a holy temple. He concludes the section by saying, "In him you also are being built together into a dwelling place for God by the Spirit" (Eph. 2:22). From this passage and others, it is clear that God is forming us, His people, into a spiritual building. For most Christians, this is not a new idea. The concept that God is building us together is a fundamental teaching of the church, one found in both the Old and New Testaments. Of course, Scripture uses different terminology in different places.

The Missing Element of Worship

Sometimes we are collectively referred to as a temple. Other times, like the passage above, we are called "a dwelling place for God." Whatever the terminology, though, it is ultimately the same idea.

However, even when we understand that God is shaping us into a building, too often we miss His purpose in doing so. We might wonder, *Why is He making us into a building? What's His objective behind assembling us into a temple?* The answer is found in the second chapter of Peter's first letter. "You yourselves like living stones are being built up as a spiritual house" (1 Pet. 2:5). Peter uses a different term than Paul; he calls us a spiritual house, yet the idea is still the same. We, the church, are being built into a house with a spiritual purpose. Then he explains the purpose for the building. He says we're "being built up as a spiritual house, *to be a holy priesthood, to offer spiritual sacrifices acceptable to God through Jesus Christ*" (1 Pet. 2:5). "A holy priesthood, to offer spiritual sacrifices." That sounds a whole lot like worship, don't you think? Of course it is! That is what we are all about as God's people. The reason the Lord is building us together is that we might *be* a holy priesthood "to offer spiritual sacrifices." The purpose for the Lord's constructing us into a temple is that we might worship Him.

If this is true (and obviously it is, since the Bible says so), it follows logically that if the building is not built properly—if the relationships are not right—then the purpose of the building (the spiritual sacrifices) will be diminished. If our relationships with one another are out of order, then God's entire intent for the building—worship of Him—will not be achieved.

Unfortunately, this is quite contrary to our normal way of thinking. More frequently we tend to consider all of the other possible reasons why something might be wrong with worship.

For example, if the corporate worship for a given service seems to us to be flat—as though something is wrong or missing—our first tendency is to think, *Well, I guess the person(s) leading worship didn't hear from God this week.* Or perhaps we wonder if they really should be leading at all. However, our first course of action should be to look into our own hearts and consider our relationships with our brothers and sisters in Christ.

As we continue, we'll see that this connection between our earthly relationships and our relationship with God is a recurring theme in the Bible. Peter writes in his first letter that not demonstrating kindness toward a spouse can cause prayers to be hindered (see 1 Pet. 3:7). Wow! That's pretty strong. Our relationships with others absolutely will impact our relationship with the Lord.

An Important Clarification

Let me offer an important point of clarification. Nothing except the death and resurrection of the Lord Jesus makes us acceptable to God. Ultimately, our relationship with Him is affected only by our accepting Christ's sacrifice on our behalf. For those in Christ Jesus, there is no condemnation. However, the Bible is clear about the attitude the Lord wants us to have toward sin. If we cherish sin, the Lord will not hear us (see Ps. 66:18). If we willfully treasure our wrongdoings (rather than being sincerely sorry for them), we are in danger of breaking the fellowship our heavenly Father wants to have with us.

The apostle Paul said, "For I do not do the good I want, but the evil I do not want is what I keep on doing" (Rom. 7:19). In light of this, it seems obvious that repeating an offense over and over will not sever our relationship with God. But *not caring* that we repeat that offense is tantamount to walking away from

Him. The key, as always with the Lord, is the heart. If we are sincerely sorry and truly desire change, then we are free. If we secretly (or openly) despise the fact that the Lord puts rules and restrictions on us—we would rather do things our own way, make our own rules—then we are willingly cutting ourselves off from vibrant fellowship with our heavenly Father.

My pastor says that grace has a catch: it's only for the guilty. He's right. 1 John 1:9 says, "If we confess our sins, he is faithful and just to forgive us our sins and to cleanse us from all unrighteousness." When we acknowledge that we have done wrong, God is always willing to forgive. On the other hand, if we hang on to our sins and refuse to admit that we need forgiveness, we have willfully removed ourselves from God's mercy. Again, it comes back to the attitude of the heart. That is always the Lord's primary focus.

In his book, *A Thirst for Wholeness,* author and pastor Jay E. Adams said it like this:

> It is true that Christ's work on the cross leads to a once-for-all *judicial* forgiveness. God doesn't haul you into court again every time you sin. You don't get saved all over again. But, that is judicial forgiveness—forgiveness before God as *Judge.* There is another forgiveness of which Jesus spoke: *Fatherly* forgiveness. This second form of forgiveness, to which James also alludes, is fully described in the Lord's Prayer where Jesus taught us to pray to the Father, "Forgive us our trespasses" (Matt. 6:12). This, He says, in response to the disciples' request for a model of regular prayer, should always characterize prayer: "When you pray, say..." Moreover, this is the only one of the several petitions in the Lord's Prayer that Jesus develops. In doing so, he says:

> Now if you forgive people their trespasses against you, so too your heavenly Father will forgive you; but if you won't forgive people, neither will your Father forgive you your trespasses (Matt. 6:14–15).

> Notice how the Lord's Prayer is addressed to the Father, and that in speaking of God's forgiveness of His children's sins, Jesus mentions the Father twice as Forgiver (vv. 14–15). Surely, then, while judicial forgiveness, determining your eternal destiny, is a once-for-all matter, fatherly forgiveness, determining your closeness to and fellowship with the Father, is not. Instead, it is a regular, ongoing matter.[1]

Let's put that in the context of this book. Several times I have said that our horizontal relationships—with those in the body of Christ—will affect our vertical relationship with God. If we mistreat our brothers and sisters in Christ with no regret over doing so, then our heart attitude is completely wrong. We are, at that point, in danger of turning our back on our relationship with our heavenly Father as well as our brothers and sisters in Christ. Conversely, there may be times when we wrong someone, but when we recognize the wrong, we are quick to repent. In those cases there is no question about the Lord's forgiveness. Again, the whole issue hinges on the heart. The Lord is apparently always more interested in the internal (heart) than the external (actions). However, at some point, that which is on the inside must make it to the outside. James said, "Faith by itself, if it does not have works, is dead.... Show me your faith apart from your works, and I will show you my faith by my works" (James 2:17–18).

You and I can willingly and willfully do spiteful things to others in the body of Christ. In doing so, we not only sever ourselves from these people, but we will also damage our Father-child relationship with the Lord. In contrast, we can recognize the error of our ways, repent, and ask God to help us change. The choice is ours. We choose whether we will help build the temple or destroy it.

4.

DESTROYING THE TEMPLE

LET'S LOOK AT the whole issue—the connection between our relationship with God and our relationships with one another—from a different angle. In his first letter to the Corinthian church, Paul said, "Do you not know that you are God's temple and that God's Spirit dwells in you? If anyone destroys God's temple, God will destroy him. For God's temple is holy, and you [plural] are that temple" (1 Cor. 3:16–17).

The Greek word in this passage for destroying the temple literally means to "corrupt" or to "mar." The Corinthians lived in a culture filled with pagan temples, which were highly respected by their society. Anyone caught writing graffiti on the walls or chipping away at stones in the wall received an instant death sentence. No questions asked. This was a serious crime. How much more then, argues Paul, will God deal with those who mar His temple, for that is what you are!

However, you and I do that very same thing when we come to our corporate gatherings of worship harboring negative attitudes or speaking hurtful words toward our brothers and sisters in Christ. We are corrupting, marring, destroying the temple into which the Lord is building us. Even if this is not our intent, we can still *unknowingly* destroy the temple by embracing resentments and speaking negative words toward others.

Read carefully here, because I don't want you to think I am saying that we must have exceptionally close relationships with everyone we know. That is not possible. Our finite time, energy, and resources require that in this life we experience various levels of relationships. The fact that there are different degrees of relationships is even apparent during Jesus' visible earthly ministry. There were multitudes that followed Him. Out of those multitudes, however, He appointed seventy-two followers and sent them out to minister two by two (see Luke 10:1–20). He also chose twelve apostles. Even among these twelve, there was an "inner circle" of three—Peter, James, and John—who were nearly always with Jesus. Further, the Bible refers only to John as the disciple "Jesus loved," suggesting a special relationship between Jesus and John. Clearly, there are various levels of relationships.

While we need to understand this, understanding also presents a danger to us. We can begin to view some relationships as unimportant. Be honest. Are there certain people in the body of Christ you have difficulty relating to? Are there some folks with whom you even avoid making eye contact in order to keep from talking with them?

After many years as a Christian, I finally came to the realization that on this side of eternity I will never see eye to eye with everyone in the kingdom of God. The truth is that being in complete agreement is of very little consequence. What really matters is that I understand that Jesus paid just as much for those people I don't fully agree with as He did for me. This way of thinking quickly changes my perspective. I can still make the choice—whether we are in 100 percent agreement or not—to walk in love and unity with my brothers and sisters in the Lord.

INEXTRICABLY TIED TOGETHER

So, you might still be wondering, *what does all this have to do with worship?* Simple. Jesus told us, "If you are offering your gift at the altar and there remember that your brother has something against you, leave your gift there before the altar and go. First be reconciled to your brother, and then come and offer your gift" (Matt. 5:23–24). Did you see it? *"First* be reconciled to your brother, and *then* come and offer your gift." Be reunited *before* worshiping. Once your earthly relationships are in order, then—and only then—can you truly offer worship to God. If there is a rift in the relationship between you and a brother, the Lord wants that straightened out before you offer worship to Him. Jesus' words here are abundantly clear.

The apostle John is even stronger in his treatment of this subject. "He who does not love his brother whom he has seen cannot love God whom he has not seen" (1 John 4:20b). I think the wording here is particularly poignant. This verse doesn't say that if we don't love our brother, then we *might not* be able to love God. It says that if we don't love our brother, we *cannot* love God. The Lord has inextricably tied our relationship with Him to our relationships with one another. Unquestionably, if our horizontal relationships with one another are not in proper order, then we cannot enjoy the vertical relationship with God. The two are firmly connected.

The Missing Element of Worship

We have seen that Scripture clearly tells us that God is building us together into a worshiping temple. In his book *The Adventure of Worship,* author and teacher Gerrit Gustafson suggests imagining two pictures. "The first is a field of scattered stones; the second is a picture of those same stones built together into a beautiful temple. Now ask yourself, which picture better describes where you are?"[1] Think about your answer carefully, because it is important.

If we are going to allow the Lord to build us into that worshiping temple, then it will take some honesty and cooperation on our part. Too frequently we more resemble Gustafson's first picture—the scattered stones—than the beautiful temple.

Many times at worship conferences someone shares Hebrews 13:15. "Through him then let us continually offer up a sacrifice of praise to God, that is, the fruit of lips that acknowledge his name." This is an important verse and should be considered carefully. Most times, though, the next verse is ignored. It is actually a continuation of the thought, but readers usually separate the two verses as though they have absolutely nothing to do with one another. Take a look at the following verse: "Do not neglect to do good and to share what you have, for such sacrifices are pleasing to God" (Heb. 13:16). The writer is clearly connecting our worship of God to our acts of kindness toward one another. Our relationship with God is woven together—like the strands of a cord—with our relationships with one another. Charles Spurgeon said it well when he declared, "Let not your zeal evaporate in some little [outburst] of song. Show your love in expressive tokens. Love the brethren of Him who loved you."[2]

Again, this seems to be a theme that recurs throughout Scripture. The Lord ties our worship of Him with our care and concern for others. From God's perspective those two concepts are not separate issues. They are completely and solidly joined together.

The only two things described in the Bible as both good and pleasant are unity and praise (see Psalms 133 and 147). Author Linda Riley connects the two like this, "Passionate love for Jesus produces compassionate love for the family of God."[3] Theologian Leonard Sweet stated it this way, "Christian love is a form of plagiarism: We repeat and copy God's love. In fact, our loving is based on faith in God's first loving us."[4] The two—our love for God and our love for one another—are so connected that they cannot be separated.

So, what about you? Is your worship of God linked to your love and concern for others? Asked another way, do you sing praises to the Lord and then do or say mean-spirited things to your brothers and sisters in Christ? If we truly intend to worship God, then we must foster loving, caring relationships—an honest sense of family community—with our brothers and sisters in Christ. Without this, we're just a noisy gong or a clanging cymbal (see 1 Cor. 13:1).

Allow me a moment to be intensely practical. Perhaps what you just read means you need to go to someone and repent for inappropriate words or actions toward a brother or sister in Christ. Perhaps you have not said or done something wrong; maybe you simply have not done what is right—a sin of omission rather than a sin of commission. If so, then perhaps you need to go to the person and declare that you will stand with him. Whatever it might be, allow the Holy Spirit to bring conviction and change to your heart and actions.

Whatever the cost to make things right, it is worth it. We dare not destroy the temple that God intended for worship. Instead, let us live out 1 Peter 2:5, allowing ourselves to be "built up as a spiritual house, to be a holy priesthood, to offer spiritual sacrifices acceptable to God through Jesus Christ." Let's willingly be a part of a temple that truly honors God and houses unified, blessed worship.

5.

Two Very Different Churches

I'VE HEARD THE story many times. The details always seem to change, but the basic story is the same. The church is in decline. Empty pews present a stark contrast to days when people crowded into them. Current parishioners wonder why the offspring of long-time church members don't attend. The church has gained few—if any—new members in years.

Beyond the missing people, though, a visitor would be hard-pressed to tell any significant difference between a service today and one when the church first began decades—in some cases, more than a century—ago. Everything looks and sounds just like it always did. Perhaps it is like visiting a historic, old house: interesting, but not a place most people today would want to live. Probably every city of substantial size has several churches like this. They may be Baptist or Lutheran, Pentecostal or Presbyterian or nearly any other Christian denomination.

The culture or overall theology seems to make little difference. The sad fact is, some churches are dying.

Eventually, in the midst of this somber scenario, something happens. Some of the members begin to recognize that the humorous definition of insanity—"doing the same things over and over and expecting different results"—is not only funny but accurately describes their situation. At least a few of the more mature believers (when I speak here of maturity, I am not necessarily talking about age, but you and I both recognize that maturity generally comes with age) come to the realization that they have a clearly delineated choice to make. There is no middle road, and the outcome will determine the church's future.

The first option is for the church to keep doing things the same way they have for years. The same songs. The same liturgy. The same pace. The same people. Everything exactly the same. To do so, these saints realize, ultimately will cause the church to fade away when they die. There will be no one left.

Aside from the final outcome, this is actually a very comfortable choice. As human beings, we are content with the status quo. We don't like change. Make any, and we'll let you know we're not pleased. Sour expressions, gruff tones, crossed arms, loud huffs—somehow we'll convey that what you did is definitely not acceptable. We *always* use the same arrangement of this song; don't try to slip another one in on us. We know all the words we'll speak throughout the entire service, and we know exactly when to say them. We're accustomed to *this* way; don't force us to do it *that* way. We're happy, we're comfortable; leave everything alone.

That is actually a viable option for many people. Truthfully, it is a viable option for too many people.

The other choice, of course, is to change. *Change?* The very idea brings fear to the hearts of some.

However, I have seen mature believers willingly give up their own preferences to accommodate others. Christians who have walked with the Lord for decades have set aside their predilection for certain music styles or specific liturgical elements in order to benefit those who are not as mature. Seasoned saints reach out in love to help those who will carry the church—and the church's message—into the next generation. When this happens, it is miraculous and life-giving, and the outcome is staggering.

Two Churches, Two Stories

I once met a pair of identical twins. Though they were in their midtwenties, they still looked amazingly alike. Their appearance was so similar that one could easily impersonate the other. They could, if they desired, fool people. Hair color and style, facial features, physical build, even many of their mannerisms were exactly the same. However, their similarities ended at the physical level. Their personalities were as different as night and day. On the outside they were shockingly alike. On the inside they were shockingly different.

Let me tell you a story about two churches that remind me of those twins. On the surface they both appear the same. They're both from the same background. The people are from a similar socioeconomic group. The pastors even went to the same seminary, and they preach in nearly identical ways. The service styles are so similar you could listen to a recording of each and be hard-pressed to tell which church it came from. The similarities, though, are only on the surface.

The first church—for the sake of simplicity we'll call it First Church—came to a crossroads awhile ago. The younger generation wanted the church to use more up-to-date songs.

THE MISSING ELEMENT OF WORSHIP

Three-hundred-year-old songs played on an instrument that seemed about the same age were just not their cup of tea. They wanted lively music with understandable lyrics. When archaic words (like "here I raise mine Ebenezer" or "naught be all else to me") were sung, they would snicker. From their perspective, the "funeral dirge music" needed a face lift. A Botox injection would not help. This clearly would take major surgery.

The older folks, on the other hand, were perfectly content right where they were. "These songs were good enough for Grandpa and for Pa and for me. They'll be good enough for you. The majority of us here at First Church are happy with the way we do things. It ain't broke; don't try to fix it."

Quite the dilemma. Stuck between the proverbial rock and hard place. Not much in the way of options here.

Then something happened. The pastor—or some other silver-tongued orator—bartered a truce. Somehow he convinced both sides to give a little. If a compromise could be reached, he told them, everyone would eventually be satisfied. The negotiations weren't easy, but the two sides finally agreed to meet halfway. If it meant achieving some measure of peace, they would try to cooperate.

So they began using contemporary choruses along with the hymns. A praise band was assembled to lead the newer songs. They wanted a sound that was progressive but not too edgy. They actually found a good blend of instruments and voices. Hymns were still sung with the organ, but the newer songs had a newer sound. A couple of hymns, a couple of "now" songs, and everyone got what they wanted, right? Wrong!

It was a nightmare. No one—and I do mean *no one*—was happy. If there was unrest at First Church before, now it was worse. Far worse. Those who previously had been content were certainly not pleased with this new arrangement. At least

Two Very Different Churches

before, they used reverent songs. These new songs sounded like the stuff on the radio. "This is not church music," they said. "This sounds like something you'd hear in the lounge down the road."

Then, of course, those who had pushed for the updated music were not pleased either. Oh, they got to use some up-to-date music, but they still had to contend with the archaic stuff. "Why on earth do we want to sing songs where the music *and* the words make little sense to us today?"

When the contemporary songs were used, the traditionalists stood stoically, refusing to participate. They were certainly not going to be part of this new sound in church. "This was not my idea," they announced firmly. "I don't want anything to do with it."

Similarly, when the organ began, the younger folks rolled their eyes. "Here we go again," they would sigh. Further, they looked condescendingly toward any of their party who would dare to actually *sing* the hymns.

It was a truce but not unlike most modern cease-fire agreements. The slightest provocation could trigger an attack. An inopportune comment could easily cause members of either side to spring into rapid-fire, offensive action. It was not pretty.

The Other Story

I did mention, though, that there was another church, Second Church. In many ways theirs was a similar story. The same crossroad was encountered. Some folks wanted change. Others clearly did not. But the way they handled the situation was completely different from First Church. There was no compromise, no truce was signed, no peace treaty rendered. Instead, they went forward in genuine love and concern for one another.

Those who loved the wonderful old hymns did not really *want* to change. Those songs were almost as much a part of their heritage as eating and breathing. The words and melodies rolled easily off their tongues. Those songs were a sacred part of their lives, but they realized that change was necessary. So rather than fighting about it, they embraced the idea of change. They willingly set aside their own preferences in order to help the next generation of believers. New songs were sung with gusto by aged voices. Those who were mature in their faith welcomed the new words and melodies with open arms. It was nothing short of a miracle.

What happened as a result of their wholehearted acceptance of the changes, though, was most unexpected and every bit as much a miracle. The younger folks, when they realized how much the older ones had given up to accommodate them, suggested that maybe some of the old hymns were still pretty good. The organ wasn't really such a bad instrument. "Let's still use hymns with an organ on a regular basis," suggested Ross Peterson, Second Church's most outspoken new-song advocate. Those who looked closely noticed that eighty-three-year-old Ethel Burgmeier had tears in her eyes as she hugged Ross after his comment.

No, unlike First Church, there was no fighting and kicking and screaming at Second Church. Certainly, some folks handled the changes better than others, but they all chose to love one another in the midst of change. And that made all the difference.

Although the services at First Church and Second Church seem very similar in style and content, there is a tangible difference. Unlike First Church, there is an amazing absence of hostility at Second Church. The people genuinely care for one another. They have chosen to display honest love and concern for each other, regardless of their differences.

Two Very Different Churches

Allow me a moment to put this into a very different context to help us understand the point. My wife loves hot tea. I make her a cup of tea every morning. Personally, I can't stand the stuff. Why anyone would even want to drink it, especially on a regular basis, is beyond me.

Some time ago I mentioned to a non-Christian friend that, although I really don't like tea, I make my wife a cup of it every morning. He responded, "She's really got you trained, hasn't she?" He doesn't get it. It appears from my interactions with him that whatever he does for his wife is motivated by compulsion: he *has* to do it. On the other hand, my wife never asked me to make her a cup of tea each morning. For years she made it herself. However, I love my wife, and I want to do things that demonstrate my love for her. So I learned how to make tea. I asked her to teach me to make it so it would be exactly the way she liked it. Now I do it all the time, not out of compulsion, but out of my love for her.

The folks at First Church compromised out of compulsion. They felt it was necessary, but they didn't like it. The people at Second Church didn't compromise. They acted out of love. And that made all the difference.

Recently I had breakfast with a worship leader in Colorado. As we ate, he shared an amazing story. At a previous church where he had served, he helped take the congregation through a transition in worship style. As you might expect, there were those who thought this change was a great idea and others who were opposed to such a transition. One elderly woman in particular—we'll call her Gladys—fought the changes incessantly. She had been a part of that church nearly her entire life and was very satisfied to keep everything exactly as it had always been.

One Sunday night after a service, Gladys went to a nearby restaurant for a bite to eat. As she waited for her food, she saw another elderly woman sitting just a few tables away. As Gladys looked carefully at the woman, she noticed the woman was crying. Gladys quickly went over to her and asked if she could do anything to help her. The woman related the reason for her sorrow: the church to which she had belonged her entire lifetime had just closed its doors. She was heartbroken. The woman shared that no new people had come into the church in several years. The offspring of the members weren't interested in the church. They found other churches that seemed to be more to their liking. The church was finished, and she was devastated.

As Gladys listened, she suddenly realized that the woman was showing her—not intentionally, of course, but showing her nevertheless—where her church was heading. That night Gladys did an about-face. She became one of the strongest supporters of the changes that were taking place in her church.

THE INTENTIONAL DIVIDE

Unfortunately, many churches segment age groups intentionally. The youth have their own service with their preferred music style. The college-age folks have a different service utilizing their own music preferences. Some churches have special services for younger children. Others have a specific service for the elderly. In doing this, we segment the body of Christ. The truth is, most churches have never really thought through the long-term ramifications of such division.

When the college kid graduates, he is now expected to be a part of the "adult service," a service that has been either openly ridiculed or viewed as dull and boring. How should he be expected to react when moving into such a different environment? Wouldn't he feel at least somewhat awkward? Unmotivated to be fully involved? The sad part is that the church has created the dilemma. Unintentionally, of course, but created it nevertheless.

Don Hustad is professor of church music at Southern Baptist Theological Seminary, former organist for the Billy Graham crusades, and respected elder statesman in the body of Christ. In a recent interview in *Worship Leader Magazine*, Hustad said, "The church should be counter-cultural. Society divides us in order to sell things to us, and what a terrible reason to divide the people of God. The whole idea of the church is to unite people. God's will is that we shall be one."[1]

He really has a point. Our worship experience is not predominantly about getting our own needs met. If I choose a service simply because I like the style of music, what does that say about me? Perhaps making such a choice implies a lack of humility and an unwillingness to consider others as more significant than myself (see Phil. 2:3). Maybe it suggests that I am looking only to my own interests and not to the interests of others (see Phil. 2:4). You see, part of maturing in Christ means that we stop thinking just about ourselves. Instead, we willingly join ourselves to others in the body of Christ and learn to love them as Christ loves them.

Elsewhere in the same issue of *Worship Leader Magazine,* Hustad said, "When a person has grown up and has gone to church and has worshiped in certain ways, and has been nourished by those things, it's what feeds them....And then you say to them, 'Well we can't do that anymore; that's old hat. We've got to have something new.' This is like robbing people of their spiritual experience."[2]

Those who have labored to build the buildings in which we now worship should not be neglected or disregarded. They should be an integral part of the worship life of the church.

What Does God Think?

Of course, we can all appreciate the differences in the two churches I described earlier. Unless we're completely callous, the Second Church scenario certainly seems to be the better option. After all, it's a happy ending, and we like happy endings. However, when we look only from our own perspective—what do *I* think?—we can easily miss the bigger picture. Setting aside our self-centeredness for a moment, though, there is a serious question that must be answered. Which of these two scenarios do you think is more pleasing to *God?* Do you honestly think He likes fighting and bickering among His kids any more than earthly parents do?

Especially when our children were younger, I felt compelled to be sure they understood that, although they could choose their friends, they would have the same siblings throughout their lives. Nothing would change that. My point was that they learn not only to get along, but to love one another. And they have. There are few things that make me more pleased and proud as a father than to see my children genuinely caring for one another. On the other hand, there are few things I find more devastating as a parent than to see my children at odds with one another. Do you know what? God is the same way. His Word declares, "Everyone who loves the Father loves whoever has been born of him" (1 John 5:1). In other words, if you love Daddy, you love His kids. As brothers and sisters in Christ, our relationships with each other are very important to God.

6.

UNITY, NOT UNIFORMITY

MY DAD'S FATHER passed away when I was still a baby. Consequently, I have only ever known one grandpa. My mom's father was a farmer. For most of my growing up years he lived four states away, so visits were usually once a year. Looking back on those visits, it seems to me that each member of my family (Mom, Dad, and five kids) greeted Grandpa differently.

My middle sister, Barbara, seemed to have a special place in his heart. I remember "Bobbie," as Grandpa called her, running to him and giggling. My brother Bruce had spent extra time with Grandpa working on the farm. They had labored side by side for days in the fields and in the barn. As a result, Bruce greeted Grandpa in a much more serious way, because he had a different relationship with Grandpa than did "Bobbie." I was the youngest. I saw Grandpa as a giant. He was well over six feet tall. My father, by comparison, was a mere five feet six.

The Missing Element of Worship

I would generally just fling myself at Grandpa. My dad, in his inimitable way, would welcome Grandpa with a firm handshake and a warm, broad smile. My mom would move quickly toward him and give him a big hug. In later years, when Grandpa was becoming increasingly frail, if you paid close attention, you might observe a tear in Mom's eye or slight catch in her voice when she greeted him.

None of the various ways of greeting this wonderful man were done intentionally to show our differences. We each welcomed him in different ways because our relationship with him was different from the others'. Additionally, our personalities are different. The differences did not divide us. In fact, they made us stronger as a family.

Is it always necessary for everyone in a corporate worship setting to express themselves precisely the same as the person on either side? Those who would suggest such an idea usually have a noble reason for desiring it: unity of the body. That's a good reason. Actually, that's a *very* good reason. As we have already seen, unity is one of the highest priorities of the church. However, everyone acting in exactly the same way in a worship service does not necessarily constitute unity. More accurately we would call it uniformity. Further, to insist on total uniformity in a worship service goes beyond Scripture. The Bible does not emphatically state that we must all act exactly the same way in a group worship setting.

Please understand that, in general, there should be a "corporateness" to corporate worship. There are places in Scripture where leaders tell the people to stand or kneel or sing together. Such experiences can be very meaningful and even unifying. My personal opinion is that too many popular worship songs express only "me" and not "we." (I am not saying that "me" songs are wrong, only that the pendulum is too far in that direction.)

Some time ago I interviewed a pastor whose church had gone through a major transition in worship styles. The church moved from a very traditional to a rather contemporary style service, even hiring a new worship leader from a different tradition. The new worship leader brought along some friends to help in the transition. One of the friends was extremely demonstrative in worship and sat in the front pew for the first of the new services. Her arm waving and dancing shocked many of the folks in that church. It was quite different from their past experience. Though the pastor wanted to move the church ahead, this was a bit too much too quickly. Some people who were uncertain about the changes became openly rebellious as a result. Because the woman drew undue attention to herself, the entire plan was set back.

Now, in some churches this woman's expressiveness would not have been out of order in the least. It would be the norm. The leadership of each individual church must decide for themselves, based on the precepts of God's Word, how far they are willing to go and how quickly they want to get there. For example, Scripture talks about worshiping God in ways like singing or playing musical instruments. Most churches utilize these expressions. The Bible also mentions expressing worship to God by other demonstrative means like shouting and dancing. All of these various expressions are acceptable, yet God's Word does not demand all of these in every service. To expect everyone to suddenly begin dancing in honor of God is unrealistic for a church unaccustomed to raising hands. Too rapid a change can alienate people.

Indeed, unity in corporate worship is a high and noble goal. However, the Bible does not say that group worship must always be expressed in a uniform way. Deciding *exactly* where to draw the line of individual expression in a corporate setting is very difficult—perhaps impossible—to pinpoint with any precision. If someone sings a harmony line instead of the melody, is that disunity? During a song about the unfailing love of God, if one person cries while others smile, is that inappropriate? While singing "I Surrender All," if one person raises her hands as an act of surrender, is that wrong? The further one probes, the more blurry the line of uniformity can become.

Again, unity is a noble goal, one that should be sought after and prayed for. Uniformity, on the other hand, is not. And there is a world of difference between the two. If my father had insisted that each member of our family greet Grandpa in exactly the same way he did, that would not have caused unity in our family. In fact, more likely it would have fomented rebellion. Can you imagine giggly "Bobbie" or tiny, young Tommy just shaking hands with Grandpa? Or what about my mom? A handshake for the man who provided for her throughout her childhood? Not very appropriate. However, if Dad had insisted that we do it, we all would have conformed. Such conformity, though, certainly would not have brought about unity of heart.

As I mentioned earlier, the Bible records occasions when leaders directed everyone to respond together in a similar manner. Such times can be helpful, unifying, and God-pleasing. But Scripture does not insist that we should *always* do everything exactly the same as everyone else.

Rather than insisting on uniformity, it would be better for leaders to teach the church that we can be unified even in the midst of a variety of expressions. Then, when people express themselves in differing—though scriptural—ways, they are not seen as rebellious or wrong, just different. And that's okay.

If we honestly desire to allow God to fashion us into a worshiping temple, we must make true unity—not uniformity—with others in the body of Christ our priority.

7.

WHAT'S SO IMPORTANT ABOUT UNITY?

NOT LONG AGO I came across a story by comedian Emo Philips. Although the main part of the story is essentially the same, I have adapted it into a narrative form and changed a few of the details.[1]

> I was walking across a bridge one day, when I saw a man standing on the edge, about to jump off. I ran over to him and said, "Stop! Don't do it!"
>
> "Well, why shouldn't I?" he asked, obviously distraught.
>
> I hesitated for less than a second and then responded, "Because there's so much to live for!"
>
> He eyed me suspiciously. "Like what?" he queried.
>
> Thinking quickly, I answered, "Well, are you religious or are you an atheist?"

He said, "I'm religious."

"Me, too!" I told him. "Are you a Christian or some other religion?"

"I'm a Christian."

"Me, too! Are you Catholic or Protestant?"

He said, "Protestant."

When I said, "Me, too!" there was a faint glimmer of hope in his eyes. "What denomination?" I asked.

"Presbycostalist."

"Wow! Me, too!" I said. "Are you Fundamentalist Presbycostalist or Conservative Presbycostalist?

"Conservative Presbycostalist," he responded, and this time he was smiling when he said it.

"Really? Me, too! Conservative Presbycostalist Church of God or Conservative Presbycostalist Church of the Lord?"

He said, "Conservative Presbycostalist Church of God!"

I could hardly believe it. I nearly shouted, "Me, too!" Then, wondering how far I could press my luck, I continued, "Are you Original Conservative Presbycostalist Church of God, or are you Reformed Conservative Presbycostalist Church of God?"

His smile broadened as he replied, "Reformed Conservative Presbycostalist Church of God."

"This is amazing," I responded, "Me, too! Are you Reformed Conservative Presbycostalist Church of God, Reformation of 1884, or Reformed Conservative Presbycostalist Church of God, Reformation of 1912?"

Elatedly he said, "Reformed Conservative Presbycostalist Church of God, Reformation of 1912!"

My eyes widened and I gasped. Then, as I lunged at him, I shouted, "Die, you heretic!" and I pushed him off the bridge.

Someone recently said that the first miracle in the book of Acts was not the healing of the lame man. The Bible says they were all together in one accord (see Acts 2:1 KJV). Now that's a *real* miracle! Kidding aside, it is sad that we would consider unity to be a miracle. From a truly biblical perspective, it should be the norm.

In one manner of speaking, unity is something we already possess. Ephesians 4:3 tells us to "maintain the unity of the Spirit." You cannot maintain something you don't already have. Further, verse 4 says, "There is one body." As the body of Christ we already have a dimension of unity. However, unity is also something we must pursue. Verse 13 of the same chapter describes the equipping that must continue "until we all attain to the unity in the faith." Something we already have does not need to be attained. Why the discrepancy about unity? Here's the answer. Positionally we have it. Experientially we must be on a quest for it. God has given it to us by faith. At the same time, we must endeavor to achieve it in practical, tangible ways.

DIVISIONS ARE NOT NEW

Let's be honest. Divisions in the church are not new. Right from the beginning of the New Testament church there were problems. Early in the book of Acts it says this: "In those days when the number of disciples was increasing, the Grecian Jews among them complained against the Hebraic Jews because their widows were being overlooked in the daily distribution of food"

(Acts 6:1 NIV). Get the picture here. Someone made a mistake, and someone else got offended. (I'm sure you have never done anything like that!) Quite probably it was an innocent oversight, but it had the potential of causing a very serious division.

Unfortunately, internal conflict would be no stranger to the church during its fledgling history. I recently read these words in the classic *Foxe's Book of Martyrs:*

> It was unfortunate for the gospel, that many errors had, about this time [A.D. 249], crept into the church: the Christians were at variance with each other; self-interest divided those whom social love ought to have united; and the virulence of pride occasioned a variety of factions.[2]

Clearly our divisions are nothing new. History is replete with stories of the partitioning of the body of Christ. However, the prevalence of divisions does not excuse them.

Jim Cymbala, pastor of The Brooklyn Tabernacle, made an interesting observation in his book *Fresh Wind, Fresh Fire.*

> I find it curious that we Christians will vigorously defend what Ephesians 4 says about "one Lord" (no polytheism) and "one faith" (salvation through Christ alone)…but then grow strangely silent regarding "one body" (vv. 4–6). At that point we start making excuses, historical and otherwise, for the shameful divisions within the church.[3]

Often we Christians act as though Jesus said people would know we are His disciples because we all agree on everything doctrinally. He didn't say that. He told us, "By this all people will know that you are my disciples, if you *have love for one another*" (John 13:35).

I am not suggesting that doctrine is unimportant. In fact, as a teacher in the body of Christ, I recognize that doctrine is extremely important. If I didn't think so, I would not travel and teach in churches all across North America. I would stop writing books if theological principles were not vital. There is absolutely no question in my mind that it is imperative—especially in this hour—that we as the church know what we believe and why we believe it, firmly basing our convictions on the Word of God. However, perfect doctrinal agreement is not the high-water mark of the church of Jesus Christ. First Corinthians 13 says, "If I...understand all mysteries and all knowledge...*but have not love,* I am nothing" (1 Cor. 13:2). Billy Graham stated it like this, "The one badge of Christian discipleship is not orthodoxy but love."[4]

A BIBLICAL MANDATE

In his book *The Joy of Fearing God,* Jerry Bridges discusses the necessity of loving one another. He addresses the issue in strong terms.

> I don't want to appear indifferent to the more flagrant sins in society around us. They are serious, and, what is more distressing, they are creeping into our churches. But in our focus on other people's sins we tend to forget that Jesus said the first commandment is to "love the Lord your God with all your heart and with all your soul and with all your mind. And the second is like it: Love your neighbor as yourself" (Matt. 22:37–39)....

I fear we do not take these words seriously enough. We don't embrace the fact that our first and highest duty in the Christian life (apart from love to God) is to love one another. We focus on "manageable sins" that we seldom commit, and neglect the greatest commandment, though God brings it before us again and again in His Word. The command to love one another appears in some form in all but four books of the New Testament. (And even in those four it is present indirectly; see Acts 4:32–35 and 20:35, 3 John 6, Jude 21–23, and Revelation 2:19.)

Some fifty passages in the New Testament command us to love one another.... How can we miss it? How can we seem to focus on everything else but love?

I think the answer is that love is costly. To forgive in love costs us our sense of justice. To serve in love costs us time. To share in love costs us money. Every act of love costs us in some way, just as it cost God to love us. But we are to live a life of love just as Christ loved us, and gave Himself for us, at great cost to Himself.[5]

Galatians 5:19–21 lists the acts of our sinful nature. The list consists of deeds like sexual immorality, idolatry, witchcraft, and hatred that we would expect to be included. Each of these is clearly wrong, we'd readily agree. However, also contained in the list are discord, dissensions, and factions. These are just as heinous to the Lord as the others. Our disunity is an abomination in the sight of God.

Jerry Bridges is right. We do not take God's Word seriously enough. From the Lord's perspective, disunity is wicked and dreadful. Our refusal to genuinely care for one another is despicable in God's sight. As in the story of Jason and Nicole—the brother and sister who fought incessantly—we break our Father's heart when we continue to do mean-spirited things to each other. We absolutely must recognize how awful disunity is.

To become the worshiping temple that God wants us to be, we must make unity a priority. This will require more than paying lip service to a concept—"Yes, we are one in Christ." Instead, we need to know the practical steps to take that will cause us to become unified. In other words, how do we get there? We need a road map to show the way. In the next few chapters we'll look at some realistic steps toward truly becoming a united, worshiping temple.

8.

CREATING AN HONEST SENSE OF COMMUNITY

IN JULY OF 2002, nine men suddenly found themselves trapped in a mine where they were working near Somerset, Pennsylvania. Although maps showed they were at least three hundred feet from an old, abandoned mine, their mining machinery broke through a wall and water gushed into their work area. The water poured in so rapidly that they were trapped. In an effort to survive they waded and swam to the highest point they could find. Reports say that they were in the water for more than five hours, but they finally made it to an area that was higher up and relatively dry.

They were exhausted and stuck twenty-four stories underground. There was no way out and nowhere to move. They were trapped.

"I just didn't see how we were going to get out of it," said Harry Mayhugh, one of the miners. They acknowledged they could only make it if they stuck together. "We said, 'We got to pull together.'" So they did.

After their rescue, Dr. Russell Dumire, the attending physician for six of the miners at a nearby trauma center said this decision was critical. "They decided that live or die, they were going to do it together."

Their determination to stick with one another pulled them through the next three days underground. As rescue workers worked feverishly around the clock, the nine men below talked and prayed together. Between them they had just one sandwich, a Mountain Dew, and three gallons of distilled water. They divided the sandwich into nine pieces, shared the soda, and carefully rationed the water over the next few days.

At a very low point, one of the miners, Randy Fogle, began to shiver and complain about tightness in his chest. He was only forty-three, but his crewmates were worried that he had hypothermia. So the men surrounded him and took turns hugging him and encouraging him. Throughout their ordeal they would hug others also. "When we were cold, we would snuggle," Mayhugh said. They stood with one another.

Ray McKinney is a senior administrator in the U.S. Labor Department's Mine Safety and Health Administration and a veteran of many mining tragedies. When the last miner was rescued, McKinney stood beside the escape shaft. He was elated beyond anything he had imagined: "I have never had one where you get them all...never," he said. "I haven't felt like that in twenty years."

The miners were determined to stick together, no matter what. Because of that, they all survived. It wasn't easy, however. The men were exhausted. Some were hospitalized after their rescue. Clearly there could have been moments of anger and frustration underground. Perhaps they could have been irate with the guy whose machine broke through the wall. After all, they would not have been stuck underground if not for him. Perhaps the guy whose lunch they ate could have refused to share. It was his lunch, not theirs. In their weakened and tired conditions, these kinds of scenarios are certainly within the scope of possibility.

However, these scenarios didn't happen. The men stuck together. They decided they were going to stay together no matter what. What a lesson for us in the church! In order to function like the body of Christ, we must recognize how much we need each other. Scripture says it this way:

> The eye cannot say to the hand, "I don't need you!" And the head cannot say to the feet, "I don't need you!" On the contrary, those parts of the body that seem to be weaker are indispensable, and the parts that we think are less honorable we treat with special honor.... so that there should be no division in the body, but that its parts should have equal concern for each other. If one part suffers, every part suffers with it; if one part is honored, every part rejoices with it (1 Cor. 12:21–27 NIV).

It appears that the early church (see the early chapters of the book of Acts) had a very different idea about how church should "work" than we have today. They shared their personal belongings freely. Those who had more gave to others. Such a lack of focus on self is contrary to the norm today, but such a selfless attitude created an honest sense of community.

Barbara G. Wheeler wrote a short but pithy booklet titled *Who Needs the Church?* In it she says this:

> For people of Christian faith, the only viable option is life together, over time, in a community that has come into being for the purpose of praising and serving God in concert with all God's other people.[1]

People, even in our individualistic society, have an innate need to be part of the lives of others. Though many will tell you that they would rather do everything on their own, it's just not true. Why else are bars and nightclubs packed to capacity? Why else do people gather around the water cooler at work to swap stories? Why are web sites like myspace.com and facebook.com so amazingly popular? It is simply because people have a need to connect with other human beings. All of us have an inner, God-given drive to be in community with others.

Wheeler added these words later in her booklet:

> When the church lives up to its charter, nothing divides its members. No one, no human being operating alone—even the most open, tolerant and accepting—has the power to be as radically accepting as God when God established God's covenant with the church. People who wouldn't come together for any other reason, who don't share nationality, race, opinions, who don't even like each other, can draw close to each other here, because God chose all of them. Because God's goal for the world is to put us all on the same footing, when we come close to each other, we come and stay close to God.[2]

In his book *The Great Divorce*, C. S. Lewis offers a picture of hell that is very different from the norm.[3] Imagine row upon row upon row upon row of houses. Millions of houses, as far as the eye can see. If you look closely at these houses, though, you'll find that most of them—the vast majority of them—are empty. The occupied ones are few and far between, scattered here and there throughout this vast array of buildings.

Further, if you were to inquire as to why most of the houses are empty, you'd find that it is a result of bickering. Someone moves in, and in very short order he has a major argument with someone else nearby. Consequently, he quickly moves out again. The strange thing, though, is that although this city keeps expanding and expanding, building more and more and more houses to keep up with the demand, nearly all of them sit vacant. No one wants to be anywhere near anyone else, because they are all such mean-spirited and nasty people. No one cares about the others, only about himself.

I really think Lewis is onto something with that scene. It is such a stark contrast to the picture painted of the body of Christ in the New Testament. As the church of Jesus Christ today, we need to foster an honest sense of community. Unfortunately, many people today believe they can make it through on their own.

Recently I heard about a couple looking for a new church. They had been very involved in their previous church, but major changes were underway there. The beloved founding pastor had left, and the church leadership had decided to make large-scale changes in the overall vision of the ministry. This couple was uncomfortable with the new direction, so they decided to leave.

In their quest for a new church home, they seemed less concerned about theological issues than with finding a place to be involved in ministry. They had been very active in their previous church and hoped for the same level of involvement in the new one. Although scores of churches were within a ten-mile radius, they finally chose one located more than forty minutes from their home. They felt that the Sunday-morning services were a good fit for them and believed they would be able to be involved in the ministry.

I tell this story, not to find fault with the couple, but to underscore what I believe is a serious misconception today about church involvement. Our main "ministry" opportunity is not to stand in front of the congregation and sing or play an instrument. Nor is it to teach children in Sunday school or adults in Bible class. All of these are important functions, to be sure, but they are not primary. Our main thrust in ministry is to be involved in the lives of our fellow believers, to be in community with our brothers and sisters in Christ. Honestly, how can one do that long distance?

Of course, I would be the first to admit that in some rural areas, that's standard protocol. The nearest neighbors are miles away. However, that's not generally the case in more populated areas. Most of the time people tend to interact with those who are in close proximity. Which is more realistic: calling a friend nearby to take you to the emergency room or one who lives fifty miles away? Sharing a cup of coffee—and the realities and tragedies of life—on a regular basis with a just-down-the-road neighbor or someone in a neighboring state? We in the church desperately need to foster a sense of community.

Working Together

In the movie *Gladiator*,[4] Maximus (Russell Crowe) is a former general in ancient Rome. Because of his consistent virtue and military prowess, Maximus is chosen by Caesar to become his replacement when he dies. Near his death, the reigning Caesar tells his son that he wants Maximus to ascend to the throne. Unfortunately, Caesar's son has other ideas. He kills his father, takes the position for himself, and then orders that Maximus be executed. At the last moment, Maximus escapes from the executioners.

Some time later, with his identity concealed, Maximus is forced to fight for his life in the arenas of Rome. In one stirring scene, the Romans attempt to recreate the battle of Carthage within the confines of the Colloseum. Maximus is among seventeen other prisoners who are expected to die as the barbarians. As they stand together before the crowd, waiting for the Roman soldiers who are to defeat them, Maximus asks his fellow barbarians, "Anyone here been in the army?" When most respond with a "yes," he tells them, "Whatever comes out of these gates, we've got a better chance for survival if we work together.... If we stay together, we survive." Immediately, the gates open and well-armed chariot soldiers race into the arena. Some of the barbarians panic and move away from the group. Each is quickly isolated and killed by the soldiers in the chariots. The other barbarians, however, stay together and not only survive, but to everyone's surprise, actually win the battle. Recognizing the upset, the crowd—who is supposed to be in favor of the soldiers—cheers for the conquering barbarians.

This is an excellent example of how the body of Christ should work together. It is essential that we recognize our need for one another. Just like the "barbarians" in the movie, without our fellow Christians, we can be easily picked off by the enemy. We need one another.

Even Scripture itself is an example of our need for one another. None of the four gospels—Matthew, Mark, Luke, or John—offers a complete picture in and of itself. All four are necessary for our understanding of Jesus and His earthly ministry. Similarly, each of us in the body of Christ—no matter how gifted we are individually—needs the rest of the members of the body. Prolific author and teacher Dr. Judson Cornwall made a great observation:

> God guards His appointments. It is not the will of God that one person be all things. The attitude "I can do it all" is arrogant and displeasing to God. We need one another, and no matter how efficiently we may be able to fulfill our office or calling, we dare not try to take another's place in the body of Christ.[5]

In his letter to the church at Ephesus, the apostle Paul said it this way, "The whole body, joined and held together by every supporting ligament, grows and builds itself up in love, as each part does its work" (Eph. 4:16 NIV). That's how the human body works: each part joined properly to the other parts, doing its own job so that the body will be built up. That also is how the body of Christ should work: each person fulfilling his or her own role to strengthen and sustain the rest of the body. Truly acting like the body of Christ is imperative. We need one another.

THE WRONG WAY AND THE RIGHT WAY

Allow me a moment to share with you two stories that contrast the ways that the body of Christ acts. One is negative and one is quite positive. The first is from Judson Cornwall. In his book *Forbidden Glory,* Dr. Cornwall shared this story from his childhood.

> The town of Bandon, Oregon, where my father was then a pastor, burned to the ground in an out-of-control forest fire in 1936. Federal, state, and Christian

organizations quickly offered relief and reconstruction to the distressed residents. Unfortunately, because my father was a pastor, none of these agencies would give him and his family any help. Their attitude was, "let his denomination take care of him." The denomination in which Dad was serving the Lord had no program in place for helping in such disasters.

Dad put the meager possessions we had saved from the fire into the car he had preserved from burning by parking it on a bluff overlooking the ocean. We drove to a neighboring town where the owner of a bar and nightclub made room for us in the back of his facility and provided food for us. We stayed there for many days while Dad was searching for something better for his family. Eventually, an unsaved man offered us his garage, and we lived there for about six months.[6]

What a shame that the body of Christ did not respond in a positive, God-honoring way. The response of the Christian community was disgraceful compared with how the non-Christians came through. What a terrible witness to the world. Now let me share a positive experience.

Not long ago I heard about a Christian family in which the mother was diagnosed with cancer. The cost of the treatments and lack of adequate insurance took quite a toll on the family's finances. The two teenage children in the family had been attending a Christian school, but unfortunately, it became apparent that the family was not going to have enough money for the tuition. The teenagers approached the school administrator with a request. "We'll come in at six in the morning to clean the school. We'll help in any way we can. Please, is there some way we can continue to attend school here?" Regrettably, the school—like many Christian schools—was also struggling with finances. It would be quite difficult to allow these two to continue without tuition.

However, after careful consideration, the leadership agreed that this was definitely a time for the body of Christ to pull together. Other families were asked to help in any way possible. Some made a one-time donation. Others made monthly contributions to help. The students were allowed to continue their education with no undue hardship imposed on them.

In this case, unlike in Dr. Cornwall's story, the body of Christ acted like a body. They had a genuine sense of community similar to that depicted in the book of Acts. The sad part is that we hold up such situations as major triumphs instead of realizing that this is how the body should work all the time.

Our society tells us to look out for ourselves. "Don't worry about those others folks, you take care of yourself." This is wrong. Plain and simple, it is unbiblical. We need one another. Clearly the Lord places a high priority on our being unified.

> How good and pleasant it is when brothers live together in unity! It is like precious oil poured on the head, running down on the beard, running down on Aaron's beard, down upon the collar of his robes. It is as if the dew of Hermon were falling on Mount Zion. For there the LORD bestows His blessing, even life forevermore" (Ps. 133:1–3 NIV).

Where there is unity, there is the blessing of God. The Lord's best for us is that we demonstrate that unity in every situation. Let us, as the body of Christ, walk together in unity and thereby experience the blessing of God.

Creating an Honest Sense of Community

My wife and I have been part of the same church for more than twenty-eight years. To us, the people in our church are family. I cannot even begin to imagine living life without such an amazing sense of community. Our lives, comparatively, would be dull and drab. Our children would be much different people without the contact of those who love them. Consistent, close interaction with those they admire has been a huge plus in shaping and forming the lives of our kids. And, honestly, it has shaped our lives also. I sometimes wonder if my walk with the Lord would have been severely stunted without the consistent encouragement and challenge of the brothers and sisters with whom I fellowship. We need others. We need a sense of community.

Allowing God to build us into a worshiping temple means that we work to foster an honest sense of community. We must admit we need our brothers and sisters in Christ. Not one of us can be the temple alone. We need one another to complete the building.

9.

LOVE UNCONDITIONALLY

YOU ARE MOST likely aware that geese generally fly in a V formation. You also probably know they do this because it makes it easier for all of them to fly. The lead goose breaks the wind, and the others have an easier flight because of it. I've frequently used this as an illustration of unity. They work together, and it lightens the load for all of them. Recently, I came across another interesting fact regarding geese:

> Those who study geese have also noticed that if a goose becomes ill or is wounded and falls out of formation, two others will fall out with it and remain behind and nurse it until the goose recovers enough to join another flock.[1]

What a wonderful picture of how the church should act. If we had as much sense as geese, the body of Christ would love and care for one another in the way God wants us to. We would stick together through hard times. Instead of wounding one another with our words and our actions, we would help and care for each other.

Several years ago I was teaching a worship seminar at a church. To illustrate a particular point, I shared a story about a husband who had left his wife. At the conclusion of the story I noticed the woman in charge of worship at the church was crying. Later, during a break, I asked her about the tears. She explained that awhile back her husband had left her. Not only had he left her, but the woman he left her for was her cousin and the youth leader at the church. The worship leader and her husband had married early in life, and he had become nearly everything to her. When he left, she was devastated. She was so badly wounded that there were times she did not show up for music rehearsals. There were even times she was absent on Sunday mornings—when she was scheduled to lead the music.

This same church had an administrator for their worship ministry. This freed the worship leader to do what she did best and not be bothered with the details of organization. During the worship leader's crisis, the administrator approached the other members of the worship ministry with a choice: "We can either ask her to leave the team and totally devastate her life, or we can help her through. Which one do you want to do?" They chose to help her through.

So when she did not show up for rehearsals, they continued without her. On Sunday mornings when she was scheduled to lead and failed to appear, the administrator posed the challenge to the music team: "Okay folks, who's going to lead this morning?" In the midst of all this, they covered so well for her that, although the congregation was aware of her situation, they were completely oblivious to the depth of her struggle.

After some time, the worship leader finally began to put her life back together. When she did so, she went to the music team to thank them. "You'll never know what you did for me," she said. "You loved me when I was so unlovable. You helped me through the toughest time of my entire life. Thank you!"

We need that kind of honest caring for one another. As His body, we should demonstrate the kind of love that Jesus spoke of and modeled for us.

Self-Sacrificing Love

Since we are all born with a fallen nature, the more intimate our relationships become, the more opportunity we have to experience the difficult situations. This is no excuse to stop loving, however. The apostle John said this:

> Dear friends, let us love one another, for love comes from God. Everyone who loves has been born of God and knows God. Whoever does not love does not know God, because God is love. (1 John 4:7–8 NIV).

What a statement! John tells us that if we don't love, we don't know God. There doesn't seem to be much room for ambiguity there. That verse is very clear. It could accurately be stated this way: "You cannot claim to know God and refuse to love others." If you don't love, you really don't know God. John continues with these words:

> This is how God showed his love among us: He sent his one and only Son into the world that we might live through him. This is love: not that we loved God, but that he loved us and sent his Son as an atoning sacrifice

for our sins. Dear friends, *since God so loved us, we also ought to love one another*" (1 John 4:9-11 NIV).

Again, John is very clear in these verses. We should love just as God loved. How was that? Self-sacrificially. He does not always (in fact, relatively speaking, seldom) receive love in return for His love. He just keeps on loving. If God waited until we had fully reciprocated before He gave us more love, we would all be in trouble. Instead, He loves unconditionally, and so should we.

I use a Bible program on my computer. One of my favorite features of this program is an add-on called *The Teacher's Commentary*. Here's what it says regarding these verses in 1 John:

> John made abstract love personal when he explained that God loved us and "sent His Son as an atoning sacrifice for our sins" (v. 10). God's action is especially striking since we did not love God when He gave Himself. Loving meant initiating action without immediate return (and, in the case of many whom God loves, without any return). Here is a model for love in the Christian community. Since God loved us in this way, we ought to love one another in the same manner.
>
> Relationships in society are usually governed by reciprocity. I am nice to those who are nice to me. Jim invites me to lunch; I invite him in return. I borrow tools from Stan; he borrows tools from me. Even sinners, Jesus once commented, love those who love them (Matthew 5:46). But love in the Christian community is not to depend on repayment. We are to take the initiative in loving, even when the ones we reach out to do not respond.[2]

A popular Christian song says that God loves us even when we're wrong. That's the kind of love that should be mirrored in our lives toward one another. The apostle John continues his discourse on love with these words: "No one has ever seen God; but if we love one another, God lives in us and his love is made complete in us" (1 John 4:12 NIV).

This verse seems somewhat misplaced in light of what we've just read. After all, John began on a theme of loving one another in verse seven and continued it through to verse twelve. The phrase, "No one has ever seen God," seems a little out of place in the midst of this discourse on loving one another. However, it really is not out of place at all. As we demonstrate love toward each other, God becomes "visible" in our midst. We cannot see Him in a physical, literal sense, and yet we can. The presence of God can be clearly seen through our actions and words—our love—toward one another.

WITHHOLDING LOVE

My wife and I recently watched a movie that, although it sounded promising, proved to be a disappointment.[3] There was, however, one very poignant scene. Arlene, the mother of a seventh-grade boy named Trevor, began dating one of the boy's teachers. The relationship began to get serious when suddenly Trevor's father, having been absent for a very long time, returned. He was an alcoholic and previously had been abusive, but he informed Arlene that he had now been sober for five months. Much to the dismay of the teacher, she decided to give him another chance.

Arlene went to talk with the teacher to explain, but it was she that received an explanation. He told about having been raised in the home of an alcoholic father who was abusive. He told of one particularly violent night when he was a teenager. He was trying to help his mom get away from the situation when his father knocked him unconscious with a two-by-four. The father then proceeded to pour gasoline on the boy and set him on fire.

Arlene assured him that Trevor's dad would never do such a thing. "He doesn't need to," responded the teacher. "All he has to do is *not* love him."

He's absolutely right. Withholding love is perhaps the most devastating thing we can do to anyone.

Have you ever heard the stories of people who have fought in military battles? They faced horrendous situations. Some were wounded and spent months or even years in recovery. Others were captured and tortured. Often they pointed to the fact that they knew someone back home loved them as being what had kept them going.

Some of these same stories have sad endings. For instance, a man who was captured and spent five years in a prisoner-of-war camp, when he was finally released, found out that his wife had given up on him and had remarried. What he endured in the prison camp was trivial compared with the devastation of finding the love of his life had left him.

Maybe that's why Jesus and the New Testament writers are so insistent on our loving one another. It's not just a nice idea. It's an absolute necessity.

When considering relationships of any type, our society's perspective is: What is the cost-benefit ratio? In other words, will I get as much out of the relationship as I put into it? What would have happened if Jesus had that kind of attitude? We, too, should look at relationships, not from the perspective of what we can get from them, but what we can put into them. We should love the way God loved, with no thought toward reciprocity.

Because of our fallen nature, it takes much less effort to do the opposite of all the things we are talking about here. It is easier to think and act selfishly. It is easier not to love. Clearly, following the biblical path takes effort on our part. This path, however, is well worth the effort.

Scripture says, "Carry each other's burdens, and in this way you will fulfill the law of Christ" (Gal. 6:2 NIV). Let's make our love tangible by demonstrating our love for one another through carrying each other's burdens. Let's truly act like the church, loving and standing with one another. No more attacking one another with our words. Instead, let's help each other by loving in practical ways.

Our love for one another must be tangible. If I truly believe I love my wife but never demonstrate that love through words and actions, is that really love? If I just think kind thoughts toward her but never verbalize my thoughts or display my love by my deeds, do I *really* love her? Of course not. Love that is genuine will be manifested in tangible ways through words and actions. In like manner, our love for one another in the body of Christ should be tangible.

The worshiping temple into which God is building us is fashioned with living stones (see 1 Pet. 2:5). Those living stones (that's you and me) need to be held together somehow. The mortar that holds us together is love. Our love for one another will see us through the difficulties and disagreements. Our honest care for each other will afford us stability when we don't see eye to eye on every issue. Without true, genuine love for one another, the temple will not stand.

10.

FORGIVE AS THE LORD FORGAVE YOU

AN IMPORTANT KEY to walking together as brothers and sisters in Christ—and thereby becoming a worshiping temple—is forgiveness. When we refuse to forgive, whatever the infraction, real or perceived, we have taken the wrong road. Too frequently we in the church act just like the unforgiving servant in Jesus' parable from Matthew 18:23–35. Jesus told the story of a servant who had just been forgiven a gargantuan debt when he encountered a fellow servant who owed him a very minor debt. Instead of offering forgiveness as he had received, the first servant had his fellow servant thrown into prison.

When we look at this parable, we may find such a story difficult to comprehend. We cannot conceive of ourselves doing anything so harsh, even if we were in a similar situation. How could anyone who had received such compassion possibly demonstrate such cruelty? The entire premise seems ludicrous.

The Missing Element of Worship

Yet nearly every Christian acts out this same scenario on a regular basis. We have received the most amazing pardon ever. Not only were we completely guilty, but we *continue* to be guilty. We daily commit treason against the King. We do not deserve mercy. What we deserve is the full force of God's wrath. But the Lord—because of Jesus' death and resurrection—freely gives mercy instead. Honestly, this is an even more unthinkable scenario than the premise of Jesus' story. How could we, after receiving the most extraordinary absolution imaginable, turn around and refuse to forgive others? Ridiculous! Incomprehensible! Absurd! Yet we do it on an almost daily basis.

Jesus told this story in response to Peter's question, "Lord, how many times shall I forgive my brother when he sins against me? Up to seven times?" Peter here was actually trying to be charitable. Their society taught that, just like modern baseball, you get three strikes and you're out. In Peter's mind, forgiving seven times seemed like going the extra mile. After all, he was willing to do more than twice as much as propriety would dictate. Jesus, however, told him otherwise. "I tell you, not seven times, but seventy-seven times" (Matt. 18:22 NIV).

Luke's rendition of this parable offers a bit more information. Jesus said, "If he sins against you seven times *in a day,* and seven times comes back to you and says, 'I repent,' forgive him" (Luke 17:4 NIV). Yikes! This is much more than Peter had bargained for when he asked the question. Perhaps he was thinking about one of the other disciples who had done the same thing to Peter six times just in the year or so since they began following Jesus. "I'll give him one more chance, but that's it." Jesus' words must have stunned Peter. "Seven times *in a day?*"

More than just extending periodic forgiveness, God desires us to *be* gracious and forgiving. It should be a characteristic, not just an occasional act. We should have a perpetual attitude of forgiveness in the church.

WE CHOOSE TO FORGIVE

In an article in *Discipleship Journal*, Carol McGalliard talked about her ongoing struggles resulting from childhood abuse. She had refused to forgive the perpetrators.

> Certainly the ones who sinned against me bore responsibility for their sin. However, they weren't responsible for my attitudes.... One day, as I meditated on the parable of the lost sheep, I was startled to realize I didn't want Christ to rescue those who had hurt me. I wanted Him to establish justice. I thought, *If Christ brings them into the fold, He has forgiven them. That means there's no punishment.* I struggled for a long time, fully aware that God was asking me to forgive.[1]

That sounds a lot like what might have been Peter's attitude. And, perhaps, yours and mine.

There is no earthly relationship into which we will ever enter where sin and failure will not play a role. That is why forgiveness is so essential. "Bear with each other and *forgive whatever grievances you may have against one another*" (Col. 3:13a NIV). "Whatever grievances" seems all-inclusive. There does not appear to be any room for not forgiving certain grievances.

The reality is that you can refuse to forgive. However, when you do that, the person you hurt the most is yourself. Someone once said that harboring unforgiveness in your heart is like drinking poison and expecting the other person to die. It's true.

If we refuse to forgive, in the long run it is we who will be harmed the most.

Trudy Tucker, one of the characters in Bodie and Brock Thoene's fictional book *Shiloh Autumn,* shared a profound insight along these lines:

> Trudy rubbed her fingers over a single spot of rust that dulled the shine of the new iron fence. "Bitterness is like a speck of rust." She displayed the orange tinge on her thumb. "Left alone, it will eat away the metal of your soul. It will weaken the blade of a plow until it shatters on the first small stone. It will consume the strongest sword. I cannot face my future battles if I let the past eat away my strength."[2]

You have most likely read the Dr. Seuss book *How the Grinch Stole Christmas* or at least seen the older cartoon version or the more modern movie adaptation. Do you remember it being mentioned that the Grinch's heart was two sizes too small? Have you ever felt like that? Sometimes our hearts can feel tight because we hold on to real and perceived hurts. The thing that makes our hearts feel better—the thing that changes us—is forgiveness.

When Jesus was dying on the cross, He said, "Father, forgive them, for they know not what they do" (Luke 23:34). What a prayer! Jesus did not reserve His forgiveness for the errors and omissions of those close to Him. He did not request forgiveness only for His chosen band of disciples. Jesus prayed forgiveness for those who beat, tortured, mocked, and ridiculed Him. His forgiveness seems far more encompassing than the forgiveness you and I generally demonstrate.

"IF YOU HAVE ANYTHING AGAINST ANYONE..."

In Mark 11:25, Jesus told His followers, "And whenever you stand praying, forgive, if you have anything against anyone." Wow! "If you have *anything* against *anyone.*" Please note what this verse does not say. Jesus does not tell us here to forgive if someone has wronged us (though He does tell us that in other places). He also does not command us in this verse to forgive if someone has caused us difficulty through cruel words or actions. No, instead Jesus says, "If *you* have *anything* against *anyone*..."

> You don't like the way they keep their yard? Forgive.
> You think they shouldn't drive so fast? Forgive.
> You don't like the way they treat others? Forgive.
> They didn't invite you to their party? Forgive.
> They didn't say hello to you this morning? Forgive.
> They passed you over for the promotion? Forgive.
> They spread evil rumors about you? Forgive.
> They beat you and nailed you to a cross? Forgive.

In another passage Jesus said this: "So also my heavenly Father will do to every one of you, if you do not forgive your brother from your heart" (Matt. 18:35). From your heart. That's the key. Correct words only, by themselves, are not enough. God always looks first at the heart. He is not interested in the lip service of forgiveness. He wants true, genuine, honest forgiveness from the heart. And it is vital that we not wait until we feel like forgiving. Honestly, we may never feel like it. Instead, we need to take action and choose to forgive.

Maybe you need to forgive someone today. Do you have *anything* against *anyone?* Forgive.

Scripture tells us, "Forgive as the Lord forgave you" (Col. 3:13b NIV). How did God forgive you? Completely. Did He hold on to just a bit of your sin, enough so He could remind you about it in the future? Perhaps He keeps a list of some sinful thoughts or words of yours just to goad you a little in the days ahead. "Remember that time six years ago when you—"

Of course God doesn't do that! His Word tells us, "As far as the east is from the west, so far has he removed our transgressions from us" (Ps. 103:12 NIV). God says of Himself that He "blots out your transgressions...and remembers your sins no more" (Is. 43:25 NIV). If you know Jesus as your Savior, He has *completely* forgiven you. He is not hanging on to some of your sins in order to condemn you in the future. Your sins are totally eradicated. In God's sight, they are gone, fully and completely.

In light of this, how should we forgive each other? Partially? Do we intentionally continue to hold some things in our remembrance for possible future reference? Perhaps we could tuck away a small, juicy tidbit about someone, just in case. No, our forgiveness should be just like God's. "Forgive as the Lord forgave you."

Forgiveness is obviously vital, but let's put this topic into the context of the entire book. Is it possible that refusing to forgive others affects our relationship with God? Most definitely. Jesus told us, "If you do not forgive others their trespasses, neither will your Father forgive your trespasses" (Matt. 6:15). Unforgiveness has the potential of breaking our fellowship with the Lord. Do you want to cut yourself off from God? Me neither.

We in the body of Christ must begin to live out the principles that God's Word makes clear to us. Forgiving as we have been forgiven is not just a suggestion. The whole of Scripture makes it plain that God's people are to be, like Him, those who willingly forgive. And as we learn to readily forgive one another, we are formed more and more completely into the worshiping temple that God wants us to become.

Epilogue

I'D LIKE TO revisit the opening scene of this book. Do you remember the story about New Heights Christian Church? Josalyn, the jilted woman, was still miffed at David. Elmer and Gloria sat in the back where Elmer loudly proclaimed his dislike for the drums. Teenagers Ben and Sam made fun of everyone. Bank auditor Robert sat with stopwatches poised, ready to collect more data for his case against the pastor. There were others, too, sowing the seeds of disunity with a vengeance.

Now, try to picture a worship scene in heaven. The redeemed of God gather at His throne to glorify the King. People from every tribe and people and language, all dressed in robes of white, are declaring together that the Almighty reigns forever. Voices are united in fervent praise and adoration to God alone. But then something happens. Suddenly, out of the corner of her eye, Josalyn notices David and turns abruptly away from him.

The Missing Element of Worship

Elmer tells Gloria that he really doesn't like the style of music. Ben and Sam see someone weeping because of God's great mercy, and they make fun of him. Robert sits stoically, wondering when all this will ever end.

I hope you find such a scenario as revolting as I do. It is unthinkable. As we gather around the throne in heaven—when we behold the Almighty Lord in all His glory—all our thoughts will be in one direction: worshiping Him. Everything else will be secondary. Such negative attitudes and actions would be completely out of place in that setting. When we've gathered together at the throne to pay homage to our Redeemer—to worship the Lamb who willingly sacrificed His own life for us—could such thoughts and ways of behaving be even slightly conceivable? The very idea is absurd, yet this scenario is played out week after week, not in heaven of course, but here on earth. Honestly, such a situation should be just as unthinkable here and now. Unfortunately, it is not.

The book of John records the last prayer Jesus prayed in front of His disciples before His crucifixion. He knew what was coming. He was keenly aware that the end was close at hand. Jesus had carefully trained these men for the past three years. Now, it was time for fervent intercession on their behalf. He was about to pray aloud one last time in front of His disciples. Of all the things He could possibly have requested of His Father, what was the highest priority?

> ...*that they may be one, even as we are one*....that they may all be one, just as you, Father, are in me and I in you.... The glory that you have given me I have given to them, *that they may be one even as we are one*, I in them and you in me, *that they may become perfectly one*, so that the world may know that you sent me. (John 17:11, 21–23).

Epilogue

Amazing! Jesus did not pray for them to do mighty miracles so that people would be brought into the kingdom of God. He did not ask the Father to give them supernatural ability to preach the Word. Instead He asked that God would protect them and help them to mature; but mostly, He simply asked that they would be in unity, that they would be one.

In the midst of His final prayer, Jesus clearly states, "I do not ask for these only, but also for those who will believe in me through their word" (John 17:20). He was praying for us! This was not just for the disciples whom Jesus had handpicked while He was visibly here on earth. His prayer was also for His disciples today who have believed through their message. This means you and me.

Now, let me ask you a question: If you could pick one person from all of history who would be sure to get his prayers answered, who would it be? Don't spend too much time on the answer to this. It should be obvious. If I could choose just one person through all of time whose prayer would certainly be answered, it would be Jesus, of course. And He prayed for His people to be brought into the same kind of oneness that He shares with the Father. Do you understand how much Jesus and the Father are one? What would it mean for us to have that same kind of unity?

That prayer has not yet been answered. The church is clearly not *one* like Jesus and the Father. But it will be answered. God is not going to—indeed He cannot—allow Jesus' prayer—which has been so carefully preserved for our reading—to go unanswered.

So, would you like to be part of the answer to our Savior's prayer? I ask this question because being a part of the answer requires involvement. Passively sitting by and watching doesn't count.

In this book we have seen some very specific steps outlined. When we know what is right, we become responsible for doing it. We could act like Jason and Nicole—the teenagers who apparently caused their father's heart attack—and wait until some tragedy compels us to change our ways. Or we could willingly follow God's Word and display genuine, tangible love for our brothers and sisters in Christ.

The apostle who recorded the final prayer of Jesus is the same one who clearly tells us "He who does not love his brother whom he has seen cannot love God whom he has not seen" (1 John 4:20). The Lord wants to build us into a worshiping temple. We can fight against Him or we can willingly cooperate. Which will you choose?

Please do not allow disunity to hinder the worship of God in your church. Recognize the necessity of unity. Foster an honest sense of community. Love one another. Forgive one another. Let the Lord form you—collectively—into a worshiping temple.

Notes

Chapter 2

1. Charles F. Stanley, "Life Issues," in *PC Study Bible*, CD ROM (Seattle, Wash.: Biblesoft, 1999).
2. Dr. Robert Webber, "Recipe for a Troubled Church," *Worship Leader Magazine* (March/April 2006): 10.

Chapter 3

1. Jay E. Adams, *A Thirst for Wholeness* (Woodruff, S. C.: Timeless Texts, 1988), 49–50.

Chapter 4

1. Gerrit Gustafson, *The Adventure of Worship* (Grand Rapids, Mich.: Chosen Books, 2006), 222.
2. Charles Spurgeon, *Spurgeon's Daily Devotional*, in *PC Study Bible*, CD-ROM (Seattle, Wash.:Biblesoft, 1999).
3. Linda Riley, *The Call to Love* (Wheaton, Ill.: Tyndale House Publishers, 2000), 46.
4. Leonard Sweet, *Out of the Question...Into the Mystery* (Colorado Springs, Colo.: WaterBrook Press, 2004), 24.

Chapter 5

1. Don Hustad, quoted in "Come Together," *Worship Leader Magazine* (September 2006): 82.
2. Don Hustad, quoted in "Talkin' 'Bout My Generation," *Worship Leader Magazine* (September 2006): 28.

Chapter 7

1. http://digg.com/general_sciences/11_Most_Important_Philosophical_Quotations. (Please do not take this quotation as an endorsement of the humor of Emo Philips.)
2. *Foxe's Book of Martyrs*, www.sacred-texts.com/chr/martyrs/fox102.htm.
3. Jim Cymbala, *Fresh Wind, Fresh Fire* (Grand Rapids, Mich.: Zondervan Publishing House, 1997), 93.
4. Billy Graham, quoted by Harold Myra and Marshall Shelley, "Leading with Love," *Today's Christian* (September/October 2005): 43.
5. Jerry Bridges, *The Joy of Fearing God* (Colorado Springs, Colo.: WaterBrook Press, 1997), 163–164.

Chapter 8

1. Barbara G. Wheeler, *Who Needs the Church?* (Louisville, Ky.: Geneva Press, 2004), 6.
2. Ibid., 8.
3. I am not suggesting that Lewis's picture is theologically correct, but it is definitely a point worth pondering.
4. Not a movie I recommend. Although it has a good story line, the intense violence and gore make it inappropriate for most people.
5. Judson Cornwall, *Forbidden Glory* (Hagerstown, Md.: McDougal Publishing, 2001), 153.
6. Ibid., 175–176.

CHAPTER 9

1. Tommy Tenney, *God's Dream Team* (Ventura, Calif.: Regal Books, 1999), 52.
2. *The Teacher's Commentary* (Wheaton, Ill: Scripture Press Publications, 1987), in *PC Study Bible*, CD-ROM (Seattle, Wash.:Biblesoft, 1999).
3. The movie *Pay It Forward* from Warner Brothers is not one that I recommend.

CHAPTER 10

1. Carol McGalliard, "Stunned by Grace," *Discipleship Journal*, Issue 141 (May/June 2004): 68–69.
2. Bodie Thoene, and Brock Thoene, *Shiloh Autumn* (Nashville, Tenn.: Thomas Nelson Publishers, 1996), 460.